BERTIE HUSTON

FREELANCE WRITER

The Ultimate Guide to Successful Freelance Writing, Learn Helpful Writing Tips and Other Valuable Advice on How You Can Make Money in Freelance Writing

Descrierea CIP a Bibliotecii Naţionale a României
BERTIE HUSTON
FREELANCE WRITER. The Ultimate Guide to Successful Freelance Writing, Learn Helpful Writing Tips and Other Valuable Advice on How You Can Make Money in Freelance Writing / Bertie Huston. – Bucharest: Editura My Ebook, 2020
ISBN

BERTIE HUSTON

FREELANCE WRITER

The Ultimate Guide to Successful Freelance Writing, Learn Helpful Writing Tips and Other Valuable Advice on How You Can Make Money in Freelance Writing

My Ebook Publishing House
Bucharest, 2020

CONTENTS

Introduction to Freelancing 9

What is Freelancing? ..…...................................... 10

Scope of Freelancing 10

Benefits of Freelancing 11

Building a Successful Freelance Writing Career 13

Case Study 13

Freelance Writing 14

How to build a successful freelance writing career? 15

Types of Freelance Writing 18

Types of Freelance Writing 18

CREATIVE WRITING – *An Art* 22

What is Creative Writing? 23

How to enhance creative writing skills? 24

Tips to improve creative writing? 25

Web Blog Writing 27

Web Blog Writing 27

Types of Blogs 28

Tips to improve blog writing 29

SEO Writing 31

SEO Writing and Its Significance 31

Guidelines to Improve SEO Writing 32

Sales and Marketing writing 36

Forms of Sales and marketing writing 36

Tips to improve sales and marketing articles 37

Newsletters and Editorial Writing 39

Newsletter Writing 39

Guidelines to Improve Newsletter Writing 40

Editorial 41

Tips to Develop Effective Editorials 42

Magazine Writing 43

Guidelines to Improve Magazine Writing 44

EBook Writing 46

EBOOK – Definition 47

Advantages of eBooks 47

Guidelines to improve eBook writing 48

Choosing the Right Topic- Limitations and Guidelines 50

Factors Limiting Freedom of Choice 50

Guidelines for Choosing the Right Topic 52

Realizing Your Writing Skills 54

Realizing Your Writing Skills 55

Inking your writing Skills 58

Tips To Improve Your Writing Skills 58

Analyzing Your Writing Needs 62

Process to Develop Quality Writing 63

How to Establish Credibility 66

Tips to Establish Credibility 67

How to Handle Difficult Clients 70

Tips to handle difficult clients 71

Finding Freelance Writing Opportunities 74

Different Ways to Find Freelance Writing Jobs 74

Freelance Writing - In a Glimpse 79

CHAPTER 1

INTRODUCTION TO FREELANCING

Introduction to Freelancing

I have no special talents. I am only passionately curious. - Albert Einstein

If someone asks you to describe world renowned inventors in one word, that word would be of course „Curious", a fundamental trait that distinguishes an inventor from the rest of the world. As cited by Albert Einstein, a famous scientist and inventor, nothing but his curiosity enabled him to achieve success. Throughout history innovators and inventors have brought novel ways of doing things and then came the miracle, the „Internet", a global data communication system. A revolution, that brought the world together just in a click. The fastest data sharing source around the globe, internet, is attributed to the birth of various new fields today,

Freelancing is one of them. In this chapter we will have an insight about freelancing, its scope and its benefits.

What is Freelancing?

Definition: Introduced by Sir Walter Scott, the term „free lancer", was used to describe a „medieval mercenary warrior", indicating that „the lance" is a person who is not sworn to any lord"s services. A more recent definition however defines a freelancer as follows:

- A freelancer is someone who is self employed and not committed to a particular employer for a longer period of time.‖

Freelancers may work in a variety of areas by sitting at their home at their own pace, selling their services on hourly, daily, or task basis, not as regular employees by one employer. Freelancing is nothing, but just a flexible way of selling your expertise and professional capabilities in the marketplace via internet.

Scope of Freelancing

The expansion of online businesses have attributed to the availability of freelance opportunities in the market, making freelancing a field of enormous demand. According to the Statistics published by the United States Department of Labor, approximately 7.4% of the US workforce (10.3 million workers) is on independent contracts. The report also indicates that because of cheap human resource available in many developing countries around the world, offshore outsourcing and crowd sourcing have also become frequent. In the last three years, US companies have increased their outsourcing by 22% on the internet. As a result, freelancing is widely expanding and its mounting scope is manifested in the areas of writing, editing, indexing, software development, proof reading, website design, advertising, open innovations and many others. With ever escalating prospects of online businesses, the golden opportunities in the field of freelancing are going nowhere.

Benefits of Freelancing

Today freelancing has evolved as a complete industry, bringing with it several benefits. A few are highlighted below:

- *Master of your own actions*

Freelancers work at their convenience. They choose their own bosses, have choice over the type of task to take up and usually have more freedom over their work schedule, which employees in regular employment merely enjoy.

- *Source of income for part timers*

Freelancing is getting popular amongst students, house wives, unemployed and part timers, who want an extra source of income to meet their needs.

- *Variety of assignments*

Freelancers usually enjoy a greater variety of assignments, than people in regular employments, which may help them increase and refine their professional skills.

- *No boundaries, No limitation:*

Freelancing is the only industry where employee and employer can work together from any- where around the globe with no legal, contractual or geographical boundaries. Freelancers may not even see their employees most of the time but it might become a point of worry sometimes.

One of the fastest and flexible way of getting a job done, meeting your desires and earning your living, the area of freelancing is very vast and not all of them can be explore in one go. In this book our focus will be on exploring the field of **freelance writing** and getting a deeper insight on it.

CHAPTER 2

BUILDING A SUCCESSFUL
FREELANCE WRITING CAREER

Building a Successful Freelance Writing Career

As discussed in the previous chapter that the internet revolution has transformed freelancing into a prospering industry. With hundreds of avenues for freelancers to explore, „Freelance writing" is the most promising one. The following case study highlights the success story of a freelance writer:

Case Study

Dr. Alice Jane Lippner the CEO of Info briefings LLC (an information marketing and seminar business), was professionally a physician and attorney. But she never got utmost satisfaction from her work as her creativity was always hindered by tight work and personal schedules, unless she began freelance writing for a pharmaceutical company in 1989.With the ultimate freedom of work, she successfully expanded her business into a lucrative info-empire. She sees freelance writing as a rationale behind her success and says:

_My only regret was that I didn't do it sooner. Freelance writing is the perfect career to escape from the - rat race. I love it. I can't believe how I ever survived before I found the solution to achieving balance (sanity)?'

But the question is how can we build a successful freelance writing career? In this chapter we will discuss a few tips and see how we can build lucrative business empires as developed by Dr. Alice Jane.

Freelance Writing

Freelance writing today is a lucrative business opportunity. As online medium has become a major source of information sharing, more and more businesses are going online. This has eventually increased the demand of content writers as any website developed for whatever purpose, must need some content in it. Also, to save costs and get focused to their primary business many people outsource content writing, bringing an opportunity for freelance writers.

Various types of freelance writing are creative writing, eBook writing, sales and marketing writing, newsletter and editorial, magazine writing, SEO writing, web blog writing and many more which we will discuss in later chapters.

How to build a successful freelance writing career?

Although, for writers to break into the freelance market, there are many opportunities but it requires skills and correct strategy to achieve success. Let"s find out some smarter ways to success in different phases of your freelancing career.

1. Start-up Phase

- ***Evaluate your skills and interests:*** It is imperative to evaluate your own self before offering your services to the market. Freelancing is flexible and you can choose jobs that suit your interest, education, skills and background.

- ***Preliminary search***: Actively search online for freelance jobs available and get your self registered with various good freelance writing sites on the internet.

- *Introduce your services to prospects*: A well designed "Bio-sheet", is a best resource to offer yourself to the prospective client. It is a document similar to a resume carrying a brief description of your education, skills, experiences and interests.

2 Growth Phase

Beware of the single-client trap: As freelance work is job based and generally no contracts are signed, it is crucial to work for a number of clients rather than stick to a single client, but ethically, you must avoid giving services to clients who might be each others close competitors.

Improve your writing skills: In order to retain your jobs it is essential to keep improving your writing skills. In later chapters we will discuss in detail how can you improve your writing skills and be persistent.

Take criticism positively: Take criticism and comments from your clients as guidelines for future success and never get discouraged on rejections.

3. Maturity Phase

Be consistent: Consistency is crucial for long term existence. It is generally observed that freelancing is considered as a source of second income and people take it very casually and get bored too quickly.

Stay in touch with old clients: Relationship building is considered as a key to success as market is flooded with masses of freelance writers from all over the globe.

Hence freelance writing is an open platform for anyone anywhere in the world, but long term persistence is not every ones cup of tea. One should take it is a passion and it requires skills and intense hard work to get success.

CHAPTER 3

TYPES OF FREELANCE WRITING

Types of Freelance Writing

Today Freelance writing is getting popular around the globe as the field is not only very flexible but also very vast and can absorb people from all areas of life and this is why it is often regarded as one of the most popular forms of self employment. Based on his skills, interests and creativity, a freelance writer can opt from a wide variety of job categories available under the umbrella of freelance writing. This text is dedicated to identify the various types of jobs available to freelance writers.

Types of Freelance Writing

Freelance writing has two forms, print (magazines and newspapers) and web content (web based). There are a number of ways through which a freelance writer can earn a steady source of income. You can work as research writers, essay writers, story and drama writers, copy writers, bloggers, eBook writers, magazine writers, catalogue material writers, content writers, advertising copy writers, corporate copy writers, grant writing (for nonprofit organizations), essay writers, resume writers are just to name a few. However, all these above listed freelance writing jobs may fit in one way or another under any of the below mentioned broad categories.

Creative writing

Creative writing is often referred to as the imaginative and original form of writing. It requires a great deal of creativity and thought to compose such artistic writing pieces. It is different from other technical forms of writing as it is guided by writer"s own feelings and emotions. Writing which may fall under this category includes poems, novel, drama, story, epic etc.

Web Blog and SEO writing

Today a number of websites are hiring people to stock content on their websites. Web blog and SEO writing comes under this category.

Web Blog contents are normally shorter than other forms of freelance writing like technical writing or research writing. Blog posts are normally written in a very informal tone and may attract many youngsters who like staying up with internet buzz to work as blog freelance writers.

SEO writing refers to Search Engine Optimization writing. It is a form of web content writing, where, writers are required to keep focus on key words and other search optimization techniques, which bring traffic to their sites. The pay is usually a flat rate and sometimes with bonuses for traffic attraction.

Newsletters, Editorial and Magazine writing

These are one of the most lucrative and technical forms of writing that may fall under the umbrella of copywriting. These forms of writings require defined focus, in-depth research and an extensive reading. It is best suited for people from the advertising agencies, publishers, public relation firms etc.

Sales and Marketing Writing

Sales and marketing writing is the most common source of freelance writing that generally requires marketing skills. As businesses around the globe are going online, companies require the services of efficient freelance writers for online marketing of their services and products. It usually involves writing product descriptions, sales letters, marketing oriented web papers and media content, marketing and business plans etc.

EBook Writing

As internet is becoming a wide medium, the scope for EBook writers is expanding. Many electronic publishing houses are hiring the services of eBook writers. EBook writing may sometimes take the form of ghost writing, where the original author of the book remains anonymous or someone else"s name is attached to the work done by you. People who value recognition in their field may find it unattractive.

The above mentioned forms of freelance writing are so vast that they are considered to be individual fields in themselves. Therefore our next few chapters are dedicated to have a detailed insight of individually each of them.

CHAPTER 4

CREATIVE WRITING – AN ART

CREATIVE WRITING – *An Art*

_Don't tell me the moon is shining; show me the glint of light on broken glass.' ~Anton Chekhov[1]

Let us recall the names of few famous writers. What names come to your mind??? Charles Dickens, Jane Austen, Thomas Hardy are few of the many finest British writers, a land that is proud of nurturing and producing gems to the world"s literature stage[1]. Now just think what was common in all the above mentioned writers….???? And the answer is their association to creative writing, one of the most famous forms of writing.

In this chapter we will highlight insight about creative writing, its forms and required skills and tips to improve creative writing.

What is Creative Writing?

- Creative writing is writing that expresses the writer's thoughts and feelings in an imaginative, often unique, and poetic way.‖ (Sil.org – What is Creative Writing?)[1]

Although all writing is creative to an extent, but creative writing is something that brings emotions and develops a sense of feeling in the mind of the readers. It is written so artistically that the reader may actually visualize what he or she is reading. *Creative writing is not telling it's actually about showing.*

Creative writing is considered as a writing of original composition. It is normally not aimed at just conveying simple information and goes beyond the boundaries of technical forms of writing like professional writing, journalistic writing etc. Works that are part of this form of writing are any fiction, creative nonfiction or poetry writing for example drama, novels, short stories, epics, poems and many more.

How to enhance creative writing skills?

- I love writing. I love the swirl and swing of words as they tangle with human emotions‖.
James Michener[1]

As quoted above, creative writing is an art and it works well for people who consider writing as passion. If you think you have that passion, here are some ways to enhance your skills and make creative writing a successful profession for you.

Get a degree

Creative writing is such a promising profession today that huge range of courses is offered at schools, colleges and universities. You can even go online and register yourself with some institute to enhance your professionalism.

Be a good reader

A man will turn over half a library to make one book. ~ **Samuel Johnson[1]**

Try to read work of well known writers not to imitate them, just to grab techniques, how these authors have crafted their text.

Be a good observer

Creative writing comes from imagination and you can imagine well only if you observe well. So always try to deeply observe everything and anything around you, enquire yourself how you feel about it and try to deposit those feelings in your work.

Only work when not at work

Imagination only works well when your mind is relaxed; always write when your mind is relaxed and unoccupied.

Tips to improve creative writing?

Now let''s review some tips that will help you create art pieces in the field of creative writing:

- *Never write just talk*

- Ink on paper is as beautiful to me as flowers on the mountains; God composes, why shouldn't we?‖ Audra Foveo-Alba[1]

What comes to your mind when you read this phrase? Images of mountains, beautiful flowers etc..?? Creative writing is about imagination. It is not about telling it"s about showing, in order to stimulate your readers" feelings and emotions, select words that trigger their imagination.

- ***Be precise yet simple***

Avoid using vague words. Select words, that means what you intent to say. For example reading „the boy rushed to the hospital", is far more meaningful then to read "the boy runs to the hospital". Always remember to avoid using difficult and complex words.

- ***Keep the text concise and avoid repetition***

Be concise and eliminate excessive verbs, adverbs or unnecessary words in your writing.

- ***Use Active Tense***

Using active tense instead of passive, it will not only make your work concise but also it sounds stronger and present a more active image to the reader.

CHAPTER 5

WEB BLOG WRITING

Web Blog Writing

As internet is evolving as a social web site with interactive communication, blogs have gained popularity. Today blog writers are actually impacting the world of politics, business and society with their words. This chapter will give us insight about writing and help us explore ways to improve our skills to enhance web blog writing.

Web Blog Writing

A „Web Blog" is a type of a web site that is usually maintained with entries on a regular basis. The distinct feature of blog that differentiate it from other web sites is its interactivity, as it usually allows viewers to leave comments. The basic distinguishing features are:

Contents or entries are displayed in Chronological fashion (reverse chronological order)

Viewers can posts comments

Other blog authors and websites may also interact

Entries are updated regularly

Entries can take various forms and a typical blog combines texts, images, links to other websites and blogs.

Types of Blogs

Web blogs are the fastest- growing means of mass communication, escalating the demand for web blog writers. Initially use of blog was limited to private personal diaries but today blogs are considered as a global social phenomenon and are used for a wide range of purposes. Various types of blogs differentiated by the type of content they deliver are:

Personal Blogs:

Also sometimes termed as personal diaries, are blogs maintained by an individual. Content on blog writing can be about anything your own self, about any idea, about discussion on any news etc.

Corporate Blogs:

Corporate blogs are used by many businesses and corporations either internally to enhance communication within the company or generally externally for marketing and public relations. Similarly many clubs and societies are using blogs to interact with their members.

Topical Blogs (by genre):

Blogs focusing on a particular subject are categorized as topical blogs. Some examples are travel blogs, political blogs, fashion blogs, legal blogs etc.

Tips to improve blog writing

Successful blog writers have to keep their minds updated as its core is being able to write persuasive and engaging content on a consistent basis over time. Some basic tips to writing appealing blogs that might be worth noticing are:

Select appealing title:

The first thing that attracts audience to your blog is the title. You should be very vigilant while choosing a title. Select a compelling title that clearly tells you about the content of the post.

Give Maximum information in minimum words:

In order to keep your content interesting, keep it short but informative. Normally do not post more than 250 words.

Link Extensively:

Posting comments on other blogs and links may help you attract audience to your blogs. But be cautious don"t just post anything.

Focus on keywords:

Try to use key words that you think people will use to search for your post. Also make sure that the placement of keywords be optimal.

Ask for Feedback/ Comments:

As interactivity is the unique factor of Blog, always make sure that you should incorporate several questions in your content that drives viewers to post a comment on your blog.

CHAPTER 6

SEO WRITING

SEO Writing

In the highly competitive online industry today, high online viewership is critical to success. SEO writing is one of the most popular online marketing tools, intended at attracting customer viewership. Let's have a complete insight on SEO writing in this text.

SEO Writing and Its Significance

The term SEO is an acronym of "Search Engine Optimization". SEO writing is fundamentally aimed at attracting maximum viewership to maximize profits. As the online industry is getting highly competitive, search engines are playing a major role in getting web traffic to your website and adherence to search engine optimization is critical to ensure success. Companies today are extensively hiring services of SEO writers in order to gain viewership. Hence, SEO writing is becoming a popular source of making extra money anywhere around the world.

SEO writers basically focus on their content. Using several techniques they put out contents in such a way that helps you to bring your articles in the first one or two pages of online search results. SEO articles are keyword focused articles that aim to increase the sales rate and marketing goals to achieve maximum profit. SEO writers see keywords as investments in their articles, as proper use and placement of keywords, will elevate your ranking in the search engines.

The demand for professional SEO writers is soaring in almost every single area of freelance writing. As businesses who wants to generate high sales would like to stand out from their competitors in the online sales and marketing wars, SEO writers can help them attain their goals.

Guidelines to Improve SEO Writing

Listed below are some guidelines to optimize SEO and website usability.

- *Know your customers*

Professional SEO writers give first priority to the customers. It is imperative to conduct an extensive research, find out what your customer is actually looking for, what information will he be requiring, and also what words (key words) will he use to search for an article or a product etc. This exercise will help you determine the content as well as the important keywords and links you can use for your article that will not only improve your content quality and also website visibility.

- *Search for effective keywords*

In order to determine effective keywords for your website you can get registered to various online keywords service providers. You can provide those details about the key points, offerings and purpose of your article and find out various effective key words that will help you generate website traffic to your link.

- *Phrases are preferred over single word keywords*

Single words keywords not only encounter too much competition but also are not very valuable, as research shows that customers today are becoming more and more specific to their search in order to save time and effort. For example if you want to offer second hand cheap furniture on your website then try to use key words as „cheap second hand furniture", „low cost high quality second hand furniture", rather than using single word keyword like „furniture".

• *Placement and Usage of keywords*

Don"t just load your article with keywords. It is crucial to maintain a balance usage of keywords and should be effectively placed within your article. It is also important to use keyword phrases as headings. Headings play a central part in how the search engines will categorize your site.

• *Linking your page*

It is significant to link your website with other related pages. Search engines pay attention to both incoming and outgoing links when ranking the quality of a website. So linking to sites that rank well in search engines can also be effective.

By following these guidelines you will get an effective SEO copy but just remember that never compromise on the quality of your content. It is fundamental that effective writing for the web requires a balanced approach between meeting the needs of the reader, and meeting the requirements of successful search engine optimization (SEO) so that a site receives traffic without making sacrifices in content quality.

CHAPTER 7

SALES & MARKETING WRITING

Sales and Marketing writing

Sales and marketing writing is the most common form of freelance writing. Most of the freelance writing jobs today are sales and marketing related. It is a well known fact that no matter what the economic situation is, all businesses need marketing material in order to hammer competition, reach prospects and win customers. Hence, your role as a sales and marketing writer is extremely valuable and in demand.

Forms of Sales and marketing writing

Any article, copy or content developed either for sale or marketing of a product or service is considered to be sales and marketing writing. Companies can write their marketing material, for websites, sales letters, sales material, product catalogues,

36

marketing copy, magazine articles, sales and marketing plans, postcards, and many others.

Tips to improve sales and marketing articles

Here are some guidelines to improve your skills:

Customer Knowledge

Selling and marketing techniques works well when they are customer oriented. An effective sales or marketing article is customer focused. Imagine yourself as the reader of the article and write what your customer wants to hear and not what you want to write.

Make your readers demand your product or service.

A good sales or marketing article usually specifies the benefits the product or service provide to the customer. Remember that people don"t buy products; they buy the benefits. For example if you are selling a security device, then list the benefits your customer can derive from it like safety, security and piece of mind as customers are not buying the device they are buying the benefits.

Good writers do not sell products they sell benefits as quoted by one of the freelance writer who writes sales and marketing articles as:

- I translate complex technologies into clear, compelling business benefits.‖

Stimulate Action

Always stimulate customers to take action. It is also highly important to encourage readers to take quick action as the longer it takes them to respond, the less likely that you will hear from them. For this you can use promotion techniques, if the company offers any, for example offering discounts like first ten customers will get so 10 percent off. This will stimulate action.

CHAPTER 8

NEWSLETTERS & EDITORIAL WRITING

Newsletters and Editorial Writing

Newsletter Writing

"A newsletter is a printed document or report, generally about one main topic and contains some news of interest, regularly distributed, to its subscribers". Newsletters normally include news and upcoming events of the company or organization. An effective marketing tool, newsletters are published by societies, educational institutions, clubs, businesses, and organization to provide information of interest to their members, customers and other stake holders.

Now a day, e-newsletters are getting rapid acceptance as communication through email in general has gained popularity over printed correspondence. Also e-newsletters allow you to add various links that might help you get higher online traffic to your websites. Hence, newsletter is a soft-sell strategy, as it is an informational approach rather than an advertising approach to market your product.

Guidelines to Improve Newsletter Writing

Listed below are few guidelines which should be followed to develop effective newsletters:

Analyze your audience first as companies develop newsletters for its employees, its customers and other stake holders.

Focus on informing customers about you and your company and what can you offer to your clients

Make it interesting and eye catching by adding pictures and graphics etc

Keep it short, simple and interesting.

Try to engage your customers by asking them to complete a short survey, offering coupons etc.

Add links of your company"s websites and other related links to get drive traffic to your site.

Develop a reader friendly format of your copy to retain customers" interest.

Always ensure a timely delivery on regular basis.

Editorial

"An editorial is an article that is based on editor's personal opinion". Editorial articles are one of the writing styles used to express an opinion about anything, an event, a happening, or timely news. Editorial coverage in the newspapers or magazines is one of the effective public relations tool. Editorials are considered a credible source as they are based on personal opinions of some industry expert and are not considered as direct advertising or marketing tools.

Editorials usually serve any of the following purposes:

1. *Source of information*: The writer discuss about an issue or event.

2. *Source of Promotion*: Writer tries to promote a worthy activity, can be a new product launch.

3. *Source of Entertainment*: The writer entertains readers about an important issue.

Tips to Develop Effective Editorials

Here are few tips to write effective editorial articles:

Do your thesis first and know your point of view

Provide facts to support your opinion

Explain the other side of the issue

Give reasons for your point of view

Choose issues that are timely

Offer solutions to issues, a proactive approach.

CHAPTER 9

MAGAZINE WRITING

Magazine Writing

"Magazines are periodic publications issued at regular intervals, containing a variety of articles generally aimed at marketing or advertising, stories, photographs, advertisements, and other features‖. Magazine article writing is one of the lucrative jobs for a freelance writer as thousands of new magazines, most of them with online presence, are launched every year and it‶s a big market for freelance writers

Magazine journalism offers real possibilities for freelance writers today. Many businesses now find it preferable to use freelance magazine writers, rather than employing fulltime employees. Magazine writing is considered a hard sell, as magazine articles may subject to rejection from the editors. So if you want to survive, you can follow some simple guidelines listed below;

Guidelines to Improve Magazine Writing

Here are few tips to help freelancers who want to write for magazines:

Select Magazine

As a freelance writer you should first choose from the enormous number of publications available in the market. Several magazines are published for specific industries like health magazines, fashion magazines, educational magazines, sports magazines, business magazines, home décor magazines, you can select a few magazines that suit your interest and for which you think you can write.

Intensive reading and professionalism

Magazine journalism entails research and intensive reading to find out what is the target audience of your magazine, and what should your article carry to make it interesting for your readers. It"s not an easy job, as editors often complain about unsuitable articles. Exhibiting professionalism is a must especially if the publication is prestigious and well known in the market.

Extensive research and plan your article

Anyone can write magazine articles, but to be effective magazine writer you should first identify your area of expertise. Just don"t write anything, conduct research, bring some hot issues, and give reliable and tempting information to the audience. Try to be exclusive and plan a unique article to stand out of competition.

Stick to the instructions of the editor

Professional writers always stick to the editor"s guidelines as they themselves are restricted by certain limitations for example length of the article, use of graphics, word count, outlays, deadlines and many more. So it is prudent to communicate with your editors, without overwhelming them with unnecessary questions. If you have a problem with a deadline, tell your editor right away. If you have a question about editorial guidelines, ask an editor. The better you communicate, the more you will get hired.

Hence, magazine journalism is not for everyone, but if you have a flair for writing, by following these guidelines you build on your talents and marketable skills, and develop a lucrative freelance writing career in magazine journalism.

CHAPTER 10

EBOOK WRITING

EBook Writing

As the world is going more and more online and internet is becoming a means of mass communication today. The use of eBooks is gaining popularity and it has become a popular commodity, even popular then the print media. The New York Times reported that, In July 2010, Amazon.com one of the nation"s largest booksellers, reported, sales of books for its e-reader, the Kindle, outnumbered sales of hardcover books for the first time ever during the second quarter of 2010. In that time, Amazon said, it sold 143 Kindle books for every 100 hardcover books, including hardcover"s for which there is no Kindle edition.[1]

On the success of Amazon.com eBooks sale, Citigroup Analyst point that:

"That is dramatic evidence of how powerful the e-book is now. What the iPad and other book reading devices have done is just raise the overall e-book market—and Amazon is extremely well positioned to take advantage of it."[1]

These reports provide sufficient evidence on the increasing popularity for eBooks hence increasing the demand for eBook writers. This chapter is therefore dedicated to give an insight about eBooks, its advantages and tips to improve eBook writing skills.

EBOOK – Definition

"An electronic book (**eBook**) is a text- and image-based publication in digital form produced on, published by, and readable on computers or other digital devices." [1]

Initially eBooks were considered as an electronic version of a printed book, but today e-books can and do exist without any print equivalent. The contents of eBooks are read on personal computer or by using the hardware devices known as eBook readers.

Advantages of eBooks

EBooks are getting so popular today as it brings several advantages with it.

EBooks are *highly accessible*; you can easily search for your required text from any part of the globe just by going online, rather than going out in the market to purchase it.

Also its availability is huge. According to one source there are over 2 million books available for download as of August 2009.

In addition to that several other benefits of eBooks as compared to printed books like easy storage cost affectivity, quick distribution and are environment friendly as eBooks production doesn"t require paper and ink are increasing their popularity.

Guidelines to improve eBook writing

• *Select a topic and make outline:*

Write what you like and what you know. Prefer a topic that you are passionate and knowledgeable about and then try to formulate an outline. Make key points that you want to talk about in your eBook before you start writing an eBook.

• *Extensive Research:*

In order to deliver sound, effective and complete information to readers you have to become yourself a reader. Also to support your text and your ideas you need to provide facts and this can be done by surfing the internet to find other articles and websites that support your ideas.

- **_Keep it limited but informative:_**

Avoid making longer eBooks as it is not usually preferred by online readers. Online readers mostly demonstrate sense of urgency about getting the information quickly. So try to avoid writing lengthy eBooks.

- **_Proofread and feedback:_**

The most critical and often ignored step during eBook compilation is proofreading. Always ask your friends, family, and co-workers to proofread your eBook. They might come up with honest suggestions and input that will help you correct any errors and mistakes in your eBook.

Even though an eBook is usually short by book standards, it's still a complex piece of writing. In order to produce an effective eBook one should employ the perfect systems, tools and techniques that work best to write an impressive eBook.

CHAPTER 11

CHOOSING THE RIGHT TOPIC –
LIMITATIONS & GUIDELINES

Choosing the Right Topic- Limitations and Guidelines

Freelance Writing is extremely vast and supple. As revealed earlier in the text that a freelance writer is his own boss. He can work on his own pace, can work from where ever he likes, and write whatever he wants to. But is it always possible to write whatever you want to right??? The degree of flexibility of choice to select the right topics depends on a number of factors, some of which are listed below:

Factors Limiting Freedom of Choice

Stage of your freelance career:

A freelance career normally starts by working with a business or agency, providing you choice on selection of your niche like whether you want to write for companies who right articles for Search Engine Optimization, whether you want to go for creative writing, or whether you want to enter into the field of eBook writing. Initially you have limited choice over the selection of topics. Your agency normally directs you what to write but as you grow older in this profession you can select what to write and what not. You also get enough experience and standing in the freelance market and enjoy more choice over selection of topics on which you can write well.

Form of freelance writing:

If you enter in creative writing or eBook writing you have better options to select your area of interest and have open choice over the topics. For example in eBook writing you can even write an eBook first and then you can bring it to the market and find the right eBook vendor online and sell your work. But if you are into copy writing, marketing and sales writing, newsletter and magazine writing than you have to be specific to write about the respective company and its products and services.

Your own skills, experience and knowledge:

Write what you know. Your skills, qualification and experience can to an extent limit your choice of topics on what you can write.

Guidelines for Choosing the Right Topic

If given complete freedom for example in case of eBook writing, choosing the right topic is crucial to achieve success in your freelance writing career, as it is said normally;

- Knowing the problem is half the solution‖

So in the rest of this chapter we will enlist some guidelines on how to select the right topic.

Choose a topic that interests you:

The fundamental rule to right well is to write what you like. Always choose a topic that interests you as it will automatically derive you to give your best in your writing as you get immense pleasure and interest in the topic.

Scope of Topic:

Before selecting a topic do remember that you are writing for audience. Always select a topic which is of interest to your readers, for example avoid writing on obsolete issues. You can browse internet to find hot topics or issues under discussion.

Your Expertise:

As discussed above your decision regarding the selection of topic will also depend upon the level of your knowledge. Always identify whether you have got expertise on a particular subject. It is essential to build long term credibility in your field.

Choose a topic on which you can find research material:

When it comes to choosing a topic, it is often necessary to carry out some research to support what you write. So choose a topic on which you can easily find research material.

Hence above guidelines can broadly help you identify a right topic but do remember the area of freelance writing and the type of article you are writing can also restrict your choice of topic and you need to be more specific about selecting the right topic to write.

CHAPTER 12

REALIZING YOUR WRITING SKILLS

Realizing Your Writing Skills

Freelance writing is today one of the quickest, easiest and flexible career to get into and make your living, but it is observed that most of the writers who enters very enthusiastically in this field, fade out very quickly. Why is that so? Why people find it difficult to retain a long term freelance writing career? If someone asks you what is the core factor behind success in your freelance career? Your answer would surely be a well developed content. No one can deny that effective writing is the key to success for a freelance writer and can only be done by a skilled writer. Writing is a passion; successful writers see writing as their passion.

This text is dedicated on highlighting factors that help you realize and improve your writing skills.

Realizing Your Writing Skills

Before entering into a writing career first ask yourself the following questions that will help you realize your writing skills

Does Writing interests you?

Writing is a passion; you can only retain a long term writing career if you have drive and desire to work as a writer. As quoted by a famous writer

- To me, the greatest pleasure of writing is not what it's about, but the inner music the words make

- Truman Capote.

Are you a good reader?

You can only write well if you read a lot. Reading famous writers will help you learn some tips and techniques for effective writing. As quoted by world well-known writer;

- If you don't have the time to read, you don't have the time or the tools to write

-Stephen King

Are you Curious? Willing to research?

A writer is considered to be a complete information package. You must have complete understanding and knowledge about what you write and this can only be done by putting efforts to conduct extensive research.

Are you creative?

Creativity and unique writing style will help you stand out of competition and retain a stable position in your career.

Can you sell your idea?

Effective writing is nothing but selling your ideas. You should play with words so effectively to make people like and understand your text.

Do you have a natural writing flow?

Some writers have natural writing flow; they just fill up pages while others strive.

Do you have patience?

Hard work, diligence and patience are core for getting long term success. An effective writer is a product of patience, and practice, practice and more practice.

Do you take criticism positively?

If you see criticisms as avenues to learn and improve your skills, you pace towards success can be enormous.

Are you well organized?

If you have a well organized personality, it would appear in your writing too. As in order to be an effective writer you need focus, clarity, disciplined and well organized effort, so that your readers can found your text effective.

If you analyze yourself and identify the presence of the above qualities in you, you can start a successful career in writing. But lack of these qualities doesn"t mean that you cannot become a successful writer. In the next chapter we will explore some ways that will help you enhance your writing skills and guarantee your success.

CHAPTER 13

INKING YOUR WRITING SKILLS

Inking your writing Skills

As discussed in the previous chapter that effecting writing is an art, a skill, that doesn"t just comes easily to everyone. Some writers are just born writers but if you don"t fall under this category, there is nothing to worry about. If you have obsession to become a successful writer, you can always perk up your writing skills.

In this chapter we will discover various ways that will help you bump up your writing skills and pledge you a successful freelance writer career.

Tips to Improve Your Writing Skills

- What is written without effort is in general read without pleasure‖

Samuel Johnson

Here are some tips to ink your writing skills.

Be a good reader:

To get effective, get into reverse gear and read the writers. To be a good writer you have to become a good reader. Reading regularly will not only help you boost your knowledge, but also help you discover some tools and skills. You can also spot writing styles of famous writers in various fields example fictional, non-fictional, creative writing techniques etc.

Be your customer to know your customer:

After becoming a good reader, now step forward and go a step ahead, be your customer. In order to sell your writing you should know well who is your target audience and what are they exactly looking for in your text. Knowing your audience will help you incorporate the correct mood and style into your entire paper to set up a distinct reading material for your audience.

Get a professional degree if possible:

Getting a professional degree is valuable for people who seek freelance writing as their long term and full time career. Even doing some short term certificate courses from some institutes will also help you polish your skills in your specific fields of writing.

Improve content quality:

No matter how well qualified are you and how passionate are you about your work. When is comes to success, the only factor that determines it is a well developed content. You should put intensive hard work to develop error proof content by following the tips below;

➢ Use clear and effective words. Avoid producing vague statements that will confuse your readers.

➢ Use active tense

➢ Talk to audience, don"t write but speak

➢ Avoid using grammatical and spelling errors.

➢ Avoid repetition

➢ Do not ever copy your text; try to be original and distinct.

Remember there is always a room for improvement:

It is always vital to get some expert opinion about your work and don"t get afraid of criticisms. Take criticisms positively and try to incorporate expert suggestions in your future jobs.

Follow a well planned strategy:

As freelance writing is a gigantic field in itself and it can take numerous forms. Each task has its own unique requirements for example writing a business letter is entirely different and is targeted towards different audience as compared to writing an eBook. So it is essential for every writer to follow a well planned strategy to create an effective writing piece. In our next chapter we will explore a complete strategy to organize the data and develop an effective content, a key to success.

CHAPTER 14

ANALYZING YOUR WRITING SKILLS

Analyzing Your Writing Needs

In the previous chapter we explored various skills that you, as a good freelance writer should acquire to polish your writing abilities and guarantee a long term success in this field. But it is also imperative to understand that given these all essential qualities, a freelance writer must write effectively in various writing tasks. As every task is different and require different solution. Let us understand it from the example:

Writing a research paper emanate entirely different tools than writing an advertising copy for promoting sales of a product. The later requires you to give information about benefits you can derive from the product, with an attracting and interesting lay out, minimal text, use of graphics, including tactics to endorse customers to take action to buy the advertised product. While the former an in-depth research paper which requires an in-depth knowledge on the topic of interest. An extensive research is required to support your facts and attain reliability. Target audience may vary from students, to scientists, to big organizations. Hence the writing needs of both these jobs are entirely different.

Thus it is now evident that the secret to effective writing requires an organized effort. In other words, you should find out, what are you writing about? Who are you writing to? Why are you writing?

In this chapter we will explore a step by step procedure that will help us identify various writing needs specific to our job and to develop quality writing.

Process to Develop Quality Writing

As of now you are well aware of the importance of writing a quality article. But the question is how? How can we develop a Quality article? There are no hard and fast rules for freelancer writers, as every job is different from the previous but we can off course follow a proper procedure to write a quality article. Let"s see a step by step procedure of effectively developing quality content.

Understand the basic need of the job:

The first and foremost step before starting to write anything is to know the purpose. You should be well aware of the purpose of the job and your clients" expectations from you. Also as freelance writing is very vast, you should know the type of article you are required to prepare. For example writing a research paper will entirely be different from writing an advertisement as discussed in the example above.

Know your audience:

Your audience is your end users and the success of your job depends on their viewership. It is crucial to know about your audience and their interests.

Brainstorm and develop a manuscript:

Before starting to write anything it is always advisable to develop an outline and format of your copy.

Create a quality content:

A great deal of hard work and thinking is required to generate a piece of good quality content. You should choose your words carefully. Express your ideas with elegance, while being direct and persuasive. Some tasks require you to call for action for example feedback, calling to place an order etc. so customize your text according to the specialized need of your task.

Proofread and review:

It is imperative to proofread the copy to rectify any mistakes or grammatical errors and to improve the quality of your text.

CHAPTER 15

HOW TO ESTABLISH CREDIBILITY

How to Establish Credibility

Masses of people around the world are jumping into freelance writing and every one dreams to become God of their field. Going from a struggling beginner to a successful freelancer isn"t an effortless journey. You might have talent, skills and experience and you are enthusiastic and hard working too but to stand out of the competition you have to put some extra to establish long term credibility and a successful career and to become expert writers whom you admire and envy.

In this chapter we will be exploring effective ways that help you to enhance your credibility and establish a renowned name in the field of freelance writing.

Tips to Establish Credibility

It is a well-known fact that professional freelancers are so busy with their work load and in meeting their client''s deadlines that they don''t have enough time to leverage their skills to grow their own business. In order to establish credibility you need to market yourself prudently. Here are some tips to attain credibility:

Avoid short cuts:

Many freelancers focus on short term goals. In order to meet deed lines and tight work schedule they try to duplicate and copy for many of the online sources. Remember this is the most perilous step to harm your credibility.

Always meet your dead lines:

It is crucial to make sure to meet deadlines. Always take up project when you are confident that you can finish then in time and never compromise on the quality of your work.

Identity and superiority

Ask yourself a simple question that why should clients hire you? You should have some superiority over others. Focus on your specialty. Market yourself well, focus on your area of specialty and promote your key skills. Remember that if you"re not superior in some way, why anyone would seek your services.

Visibility

You might be efficient and effective freelance writer but how can clients hire you if they can"t see you. You have to be visible and accessible. This can be done by

- Getting involved in your professional community
- Writing articles
- Develop and update your own website
- Always be in touch with your old clients
- Develop and update your blog

The following comments made by a successful freelancer on the benefits of blogging are posted below:

In her post, *"Why I Write this Blog,"* freelancer P.S. Jones says that blogging is a way for her to remain accountable and meet virtual colleagues. When you think of it in these terms, you can"t deny that your blog is an important part of your freelance businesses. If you write well, each and every one of your posts can generate new leads and help showcase your skills and services around the clock.

Tough in this chapter we have explored several ways of attaining credibility in the market but nothing is as worthy as an effective content. Always remember "Do Not Compromise on Your Work"

CHAPTER 16

HOW TO HANDLE DIFFICULT CLIENTS

How to Handle Difficult Clients

Freelancing as any other industry is client oriented. Although freelance writers are considered as boss of their own destiny and freelancing jobs are flexible but it too has it own limitations. Freelancers are of course bound by their clients. They have deadlines to meet and certain instructions to follow. The one other crucial aspect of freelancing is working with agents. There are many channels of communication between a free lancer and the end user of the article. This may lead to communication gap which may create problems. Also as freelancers work for a number of clients at the same time they have to face the difficulty of handling all sorts of clients and the difficult clients are a pain to work with.

Freelancers should realize that every client is different. Some clients are difficult as:

They keep changing project specifications.

Are reluctant to trust you

Keep on sending tight deadlines

Asks you for regular updates which is sometimes obstructing

Complains constantly and never gets satisfied

Paying less

Threatening you to skip to another writer

Provide you vague instructions as they are not clear of what they want.

Over powering and wants to get control

These are some aspects of that effect your efficiency. In the rest of this chapter we will explore some ideas to deal with difficult clients effectively.

Tips to handle difficult clients

- *Never lose temper:*

It is always recommended to keep a cool head. Don"t get offensive if some clients are pushing you because of excessive work load or dead line pressures. Speak to them calmly and assure them of time delivery of your work. Build an air of trust.

- ***Try to keep record of every interaction between you and your client:***

Although it is not practically feasible especially when you are dealing with a number of clients with smaller projects, but try to keep records of the emails to avoid misunderstandings and arguments in the future.

- ***Always update your client:***

It is important to constantly update your client as you progress. Make sure your client knows everything and agrees to everything. This way whenever your client says something contradictory you can immediately remind him of what he instructed earlier. Updating your client will also save you from the hustle of redoing the whole task again in case of any misunderstanding of instructions by you.

- ***Respond spontaneously:***

It is crucial and ethical to respond promptly whenever you find any difficulty in finishing your task. You must realize that your client is also responsible to someone and he has his own deadlines to meet to establish his credibility.

- *Learn when to say NO:*

Clients are off course backbones for your success but it doesn"t mean that they are always right. It is important that you should decline to any instruction if you don"t feel comfortable. But never get rude, by just saying no. Explain those reasons and present alternative solution.

- *Hear them out:*

Remember your clients are usually more experience in their field. Never take their suggestions negatively. Their instruction might prove to be beneficial for you.

Remember that word of mouth is crucial for your success. If you work effectively and maintain better relations with your clients, you will soon get known and escalate up in your career.

CHAPTER 17

FINDING FREELANCE WRITING
OPPORTUNITIES

Finding Freelance Writing Opportunities

Internet revolution has brought flourishing opportunities for freelance writers. One of the efficient, fastest and cost-effective means for the employers and at the same time one of the lucrative and flexible source of income for the writers, freelancing industry has expanded to its widest in the present era. But the question is how to find lucrative freelance writing jobs in the market.

Different Ways to Find Freelance Writing Jobs

There are a number of ways which we are going to explore in this chapter to find online writing jobs for freelancers, but a word of caution for you is to beware of scams and fraudulent employers.

Always research well and be prudent in selecting the right job and the right people.

List below are several ways to locate freelance writing jobs. Some of these options are free and others require that you pay a membership fee. All of them, however, have the potential of helping you find jobs.

Websites:

There is huge number of websites that provides you with freelance job listening. Craigslist.com is a one the best and free place to find freelance work. There are job listings posted daily. Other available free websites are getafreelancer.com, rentacoder.com, monster.com, but their reliability is lower.

However there are few paid sites that are more reliable for example guru.com, Ifreelance.com, elance.com.

Social Media Sites:

Famous social media sites like face book, twitter, LinkedIn also help you in job search, but again the reliability is questionable.

Email marketing:

For tyro writers daily emails may also work. But it is most effective for people already in the field and if they have a lull in work schedule, as happens to almost every freelancer at some point. Sending out emails to existing clients is effective.

Solicit references:

Enquire from your friends, family members and colleagues for reliable employers. These sources are more reliable and trust worthy. Even many people looking to hire a freelance writer will ask someone they know for a referral so keeping in touch with friends, colleagues proves to be beneficial.

Registering with professional organizations:

This strategy works best for professionals. Writers who specialize in areas such as marketing, medical, or technical writing could join organizations specific to those industries.

Alternative approach- Market yourself:

This is the you turn approach for which you do your work first i.e. prepare your article first and then email it to various related businesses and people who might be interested in your work and get you a freelancing job. Or you might submit your articles to various free directors and solicit work.

Create your own blog or websites to market yourself:

This is the most effective approach for professional freelance writers. You can update your blog or web sites and present your work and market your specialties which will help you to get work of your choice.

Hence, there are a variety of ways through which freelance writers can find opportunities and there is no one best method for everyone. Some freelancers are novice, others experienced, some are better at online networking, while others are more proficient at talking with people face-to-face, some see freelancing as a source of additional income while others want desire to take it as a long term profession. One thing is sure, freelance market is full of opportunities, one just needs to be prudent finding them.

CHAPTER 18

FREELANCE WRITING IN A GLIMPSE

Freelance Writing - In a Glimpse

In our journey through this book we have explored the rising world of *Freelance Writing*, an emerging profession, whose birth can be attributed to the internet revolution of the present era. Bringing with it an avenue of opportunities, freelance writing is the most flexible profession which has spread its feathers in almost every other industry including media, pharmaceutical, research and development, education, all sorts of businesses, NGO"s, journalism are just to name a few.

Freelance writers have freedom to choose their work and time schedule and they usually enjoy a variety of assignments from as simple as a marketing or sales articles to complex as research papers, eBooks etc. Although normally considered to be a source extra income, freelance writing can be adopted as a fulltime profession for people who see writing as their passion. In order to achieve success writers should exhibit persistence, consistency, firm focus on meeting deadlines and professionalism to knock off competition and gain market recognition.

We have also highlighted tips through which writer can improve their writing skills and also explored several effective ways by which freelance writer can market their selves. The text also highlighted some sources from which novice freelance writers can find job opportunities. Hence we have tried to cover every aspect of freelance writing in our text and hope it has perked up your horizon and understanding of the field of freelance writing.

Printed by Libri Plureos GmbH in Hamburg,
Germany